William Watson

The purple East

A series of sonnets on England's desertion of Armenia

William Watson

The purple East
A series of sonnets on England's desertion of Armenia

ISBN/EAN: 9783337291174

Printed in Europe, USA, Canada, Australia, Japan

Cover: Foto ©ninafisch / pixelio.de

More available books at **www.hansebooks.com**

The Purple East

A Series of Sonnets on England's
Desertion of Armenia

BY
WILLIAM WATSON

CHICAGO : STONE & KIMBALL
LONDON : JOHN LANE
MDCCCXCVI

Contents

Preface

A WORD as to the origin of these Son-
nets may perhaps be expedient. The
first of them, "The Turk in Armenia," was
published as long ago as March 2, 1895,
during the Premiership of Lord Rosebery;
was subsequently included in the Author's
latest volume of verse; and is here reprinted
with some alteration. The occcasion of
the one entitled "Repudiated Responsibil
ity" was a recent public utterance of the
Chancellor of the Exchequer. This, and
its companion pieces, with the exception of
three, which now see the light for the first
time, were contributed in rapid succes-
sion to the *Westminster Gazette*, during
December and January, 1895–6; several
have since undergone considerable revi-
sion. After the publication of the first

seven there appeared a reply, from the
pen of the present Poet Laureate, in
the shape of three sonnets, entitled a " A
Vindication of England," and addressed to
" To the Author of 'The Purple East.' "
Their substance may with perfect truth and
fairness be recapitulated in a few words of
prose. The Poet Laureate assured me—
Firstly, that whosoever in any circumstances
arraigns this country for anything that she
may do or leave undone, thereby covers
himself with shame; secondly, that although
the continued torture, rape, and massacre of
a Christian people under the eyes of a
Christian continent may be a lamentable
thing, it is best to be patient, seeing that
the patience of God Himself can never be
exhausted; and thirdly, that if I were but
with him in his pretty country-house, were
but comfortably seated "by the yule-log's
blaze," and joining with him in seasonable
conviviality, the enigmas of Providence and
the whole mystery of things would presently

become transparent to me, and more especially after "drinking to England," I should be enabled to understand that "she bides her hour behind the bastioned brine." To the Laureate's amiable effusion, with its conventional patriotism and its absolute penury of argument, pages 31-4 of this booklet are of the nature of a reply.

Passing to less personal issues, I myself have but little hope that any mere written word can bear visible fruit, while the spiritual frost lies so hard upon the land as at this time. I am indeed loth to go so far as the great Painter who suffers my pen to be ennobled by temporary association with his pencil, and who has expressed to me his belief that "nothing at this moment is possible except a national mourning." With profound veneration for the genius that has so often transferred the poet's emotion and the mystic's vision in the splendours of colour and form, I must hope that herein at least he is wrong; that something besides lamentation alone is even yet possible: though I, too, feel that *without* it — without penitent tears for our tragic errors as the first condition of effort — nothing that is worth the doing can be done.

In the sphere of practical action, if, notwithstanding our paramount naval power, notwithstanding the moral support, and surely, in such a cause, and in eventual emergency, the material support of all the nobler elements of Anglo-Saxon civilisation throughout the world, the position of England relatively to the European imbroglio and to her own Egyptian, South African, and American complications be really such as to render hopeless any Crusade of this Empire against that Vicegerency of Hell which is acquiesced in as the Ottoman Government, then let us do what many earnest-minded Englishmen, even among those who are no enthusiastic friends of Russia, are urging as the only possible solution of a problem that cries aloud, with the tongues of thrice a hundred thousand martyrs, to be solved. If in very truth England herself cannot move — if she must perforce sit like the victim of the wand of Comus, her nerves

> "Chained up in alabaster,
> And she a statue, or as Daphne was,
> Root-bound, that fled Apollo" —

then let her at least abandon her selfish obstruction of those who can move and who would. And if an appeal to the national conscience is vain, let us fall back for a moment upon lower ethical considerations, and ask ourselves whether in the end it will even *advantage* us to have postponed the rescue of a dying people to our own alleged interests in the maintenance of a diabolical tyranny. To have been the accessory to a tremendous crime, whether before or after the fact, whether by direct complicity or by the passive connivance of non-intervention where effective intervention was possible, will not permanently aid a nation, any more than it would aid an individual to go about the business of life with that inmost self-approval which can afford to ignore the adverse judgments of the half-informed, and which is more potent than any plaudits to sustain and secretly inspire. Wanting that silent ratification, unfortified by that inward sanction, a nation must needs lose vigour and assurance. Her walk grows feverish, and her rejoicings troubled, for a shadowy accuser waylays her footsteps, and haunts the background of her feasts.

WILLIAM WATSON.

The Purple East

The Turk in Armenia

WHAT profits it, O England, to prevail
      In camp and mart and council,
   and bestrew
With argosies thy oceans, and renew
With tribute levied on each golden gale
Thy treasuries, if thou canst hear the wail
Of women martyred by the turbaned crew
Whose tenderest mercy was the sword
      that slew,
And lift no hand to wield the purging
   flail ?
We deemed of old thou held'st a charge
   from Him
Who watches girdled by His seraphim,

To smite the wronger with thy destined
   rod.
Wait'st thou His sign?   Enough, the un-
   answered cry
Of virgin souls for vengeance, and on
   high
The gathering blackness of the frown of
   God!

Craven England

NEVER, O craven England, nevermore
Prate thou of generous effort, right-
eous aim!
Betrayer of a people, know thy shame
Summer hath passed, and Autumn's thresh-
ing floor
Been winnowed; Winter at Armenia's door
Snarls like a wolf; and still the sword
and flame
Sleep not; *thou only* sleepest; and the same
Cry unto heaven ascends as heretofore;
The guiltless perish, and no man regards;
And sunk in ease, and lost to noble pride,
Stirred by no clarion blowing loud and
wide,

Thy sons forgot what Truth and Honour
    meant,
And, day by day, to sit among the shards
Of broken faith are miserably content.

The Price of Prestige

YOU in high places; you that drive the
steeds
Of empire; you that say unto our hosts,
"Go thither," and they go; and from our
coasts
Bid sail the squadrons, and they sail, their
deeds
Shaking the world: lo! from a land that
pleads
For mercy where no mercy is, the ghosts
Look in upon you faltering at your posts—
Upbraid you parleying while a people bleeds
To death. What stays the thunder in
your hand?

A fear for England? Can her pillared
    fame
Only on faith forsworn securely stand,
On faith forsworn that murders babes and
    men?
Are such the terms of Glory's tenure?
    Then
Fall her accursed greatness, in God's name!

How Long?

HEAPED in their ghastly graves they lie, the breeze
Sickening o'er fields where others vainly wait
For burial: and the butchers keep high state
In silken palaces of perfumed ease.
The panther of the desert, matched with these,
Is pitiful; beside their lust and hate,
Fire and the plague-wind are compassionate,
And soft the deadliest fangs of ravening seas.
How long shall they be borne? Is not the cup

Of crime yet full? Doth devildom still
  lack

Some consummating crown, that we hold
  back

The scourge, and in Christ's borders give
  them room?

How long shall they be borne, O Eng-
  land? Up

Tempest of God, and sweep them to their
  doom!

Repudiated Responsibility

I HAD not thought to hear it voiced so
plain,
Uttered so forthright, on their lips who steer
This nation's course: I had not thought to
hear
That word re-echoed by an English thane,
Guilt's maiden speech when first a man
lay slain,
"Am I my brother's keeper?" Yet full
near
It sounded, and the syllables rang clear
As the immortal rhetoric of Cain.
"Wherefore should *we*, sirs, more than
they — or they —
Unto these helpless reach a hand to save?"

An English thane, in this our English air,
Speaking for England? Then indeed her
    day
Slopes to its twilight, and for Honour there
Is needed but a requiem, and a grave.

England to America

O TOWERING Daughter, Titan of the
West,
Behind a thousand leagues of foam secure;
Thou toward whom our inmost heart is pure
Of ill intent; although thou threatenest
With most unfilial hand thy mother's breast,
Not for one breathing-space may Earth
endure
The thought of War's intolerable cure
For such vague pains as vex to-day thy
rest!
But if thou hast more strength than thou
canst spend
In tasks of Peace, and find'st her yoke
too tame,

Help us to smite the cruel, to befriend
The succourless, and put the false to shame.
So shall the ages laud thee, and thy name
Be lovely among nations to the end.

A Birthday

IT is the birthday of the Prince of Peace :
Full long ago He lay with steeds in
stall,
And universal Nature heard through all
Her borders that the reign of Pan must
cease.
The fatness of the land, the earth's increase,
Cumbers the board ; the holly hangs in
hall ;
Somewhat of her abundance Wealth lets
fall ;
It is the birthday of the Prince of Peace.
The dead rot by the wayside ; the unblest
Who live, in caves and desert mountains
lurk

Trembling, his foldless flock, shorn of their
    fleece.
Women in travail, babes that suck the
    breast,
Are spared not. Famine hurries to her
    work,
It is the birthday of the Prince of Peace.

The Tired Lion

SPEAK once again, with that great note
    of thine,
Hero withdrawn from Senates and their
    sound
Unto thy home by Cambria's northern
    bound,
Speak once again, and wake a world supine.
Not always, not in all things, was it mine
To follow where thou led'st : but who hath
    found
Another man so shod with fire, so crowned
With thunder, and so armed with wrath
    divine ?
Lift up thy voice once more ! The nation's
    heart

Is cold as Anatolia's mountain snows.
Oh, from these alien paths of base repose
Call back thy England, ere thou too de-
    part —
Ere, on some secret mission, thou too start
With silent footsteps, whither no man
    knows.

The Bard-in-Waiting

TREACHERY'S apologist, whose num-
    bers rung
But yesterday, remonstrant in my ear;
Thou to whom England seems a mistress
    dear,
Insatiable of honey from thy tongue:
Because I crouch not fawning slaves among,
How is my service proved the less sincere?
Have not I also deemed her without peer?
Her beauty have not I too seen and sung?
But for the love I bore her lofty ways,
What were to me her stumblings and her
    slips?
And lovely is she still, her maiden lips

Pressed to the lips whose foam around her
    plays!
But on her brow's benignant star whose rays
Lit them that sat in darkness, lo! the
    eclipse.

Leisured Justice

"SHE bides her hour." And must I
then believe
That when the day of peril is o'erpast,
She who was great because so oft she cast
All thought of peril to the waves that heave
Against her feet, shall greatly undeceive
Her purblind son who dreamed she shrank
aghast
From Duty's signal, and shall act at last,
When there is naught remaining to re-
trieve?
At last! when the last altar is defiled,
And there are no more maidens to de-
flower—

When the last mother folds with famished
 arms
To her dead bosom her last butchered
 child—
Then shall our England, throned beyond
 alarms,
Rise in her might! Till then, "she bides
 her hour."

The Plague of Apathy

NO tears are left; we have quickly
     spent that store!

Indifference like a dewless night hath come.

From wintry sea to sea the land lies numb.

With palsy of the spirit stricken sore,

The land lies numb from iron shore to
     shore.

The unconcerned, they flourish: loud are
     some,

And without shame. The multitude stand
     dumb.

The England that we vaunted is no more.

Only the witling's sneer, the worldling's
     smile,

The weakling's tremors, fail him not who
    fain

Would rouse to noble deed. And all the
    while,

A homeless people, in their mortal pain,

Toward one far and famous ocean isle

Stretch hands of prayer, and stretch those
    hands in vain.

The Knell of Chivalry

O VANISHED morn of crimson and of
    gold,
O youth and roselight and romance, wherein
I read of paynim and of paladin,
And beauty snatched from ogre's dun-
    geoned hold!
Ever the recreant would in dust be rolled,
Ever the true knight in the joust would win.
Ever the scaly shape of monstrous Sin
At last lie vanquished, fold on writhing
    fold.
Was it all false, that world of princely
    deeds,
The splendid quest, the good fight ringing
    clear ?

Yonder the Dragon ramps with fiery gorge,
Yonder the victim faints and gasps and
　　bleeds ;
But in his merry England our St. George
Sleeps a base sleep beside his idle spear.

A Trial of Orthodoxy

THE clinging children at their mother's
    knee
Slain; and the sire and kindred one by one
Flayed or hewn piecemeal; and things
    nameless done,
Not to be told: while imperturbably
The nations gaze, where Rhine unto the sea,
Where Seine and Danube, Thames and
    and Tiber run,
And where great armies glitter in the sun,
And great kings rule, and man is boasted
    free !
What wonder if yon torn and naked throng
Should doubt a Heaven that seems to wink
    and nod,

And having moaned at noontide, "Lord,
    how long?"
Should cry, "Where hidest Thou?" at
    evenfall
At midnight, "Is he deaf and blind, our
    God?"
And ere day dawn, "Is He indeed, at all?"

"If"

YEA, if ye could not, though ye would,
    lift hand—
Ye halting leaders—to abridge Hell's reign,
If, for some cause ye may not yet make
    plain,
Yearning to strike, ye stood as one may
    stand
Who in a nightmare sees a murder planned
And hurrying to its issue, and though fain
To stay the knife, and fearless, must remain
Madly inert, held fast by ghostly band;—
If such your plight, most hapless ye of
    of men!
But if ye could and would not, oh, what plea,

Think ye, shall stead you at your trial, when
The thunder-cloud of witnesses shall loom,
With ravished childhood on the seat of
    doom,
At the Assizes of Eternity?

A Hurried Funeral

A LITTLE deeper, sexton.   You forget,
    She you would bury 'neath so thin
   a crust
Of loam, was fiery-souled, and ev'n in dust
She may lie restless, she may toss and fret,
Nay, she might break a seal too lightly set,
And vex, unmannerly, our ease !   She must
Beneath no lack of English earth lie thrust,
Would we unhaunted sleep !   Nay, deeper
    yet.
Quick, friend, the cortège comes.   There —
    that will serve ;
Deep enough now ; and thou'lt need all thy
    nerve,

A Hurried Funeral

If, in her coffin, at the last, amid
The mourners in the customary suits,
And to the scandal of these decent mutes,
This corpse of England's Honour burst
    the lid!

A Wondrous Likeness

STILL on Life's loom, the infernal warp
   and weft
Woven each hour! Still, in august renown,
A great realm watching, under God's great
   frown!
Ever the same! The little children cleft
In twain: the little tender maidens reft
Of maidenhood! And through a little town
A stranger journeying, wrote this record
   down,
"In all the place there was not one man
   left."
O friend, the sudden lightning of whose pen
Makes Horror's countenance visible **afar,**

And Desolation's face familiar,
I think this very England of my ken
Is wondrous like that little town, where are
In all the streets and houses no more men.

Starving Armenia

Open your hearts, ye clothed from head
    to feet,
Ye housed and whole who listen to the cry
Of them that not yet slain and mangled lie,
Only despoiled of all that made life sweet—
Only left bare to snow and wind and sleet,
And roofless to the inhospitable sky;
Give them of your abundance, lest they die
And famine make this mighty woe complete;
And lest if truly, as your creed aver,
A day of reckoning come, it be your lot
To hear the voice of the uprisen dead:
"We were the naked whom ye covered not,
The sick to whom ye did not minister,
And the anhungered whom ye gave not
    bread."

Last Word

AND save to mourn, is there nought left to do,

Nought *ye* can do, O sons of England ?
    Yes :

Ye can arise, reclaim your manliness,

And flee the things that are unmaking you.

Still in your midst there dwells a remnant, who

Love not an unclean Art, a Stage no less

Unclean, a gibing and reviling Press,

A febrile Muse, and Fiction febrile too.

And they it is would pluck you from this slime

Whereof the rank miasma clouds your brain

With sloth that slays and torpor that is
    crime

Till ye can feel nought keenly, see nought
    plain.

Hearken their call, and heed, while yet is
    time,

Lest ye be lulled too deep to wake again.

www.ingramcontent.com/pod-product-compliance
Lightning Source LLC
Chambersburg PA
CBHW021437090426
42739CB00009B/1524